God Bless

Jim Littlepage
The Fine poet

merry Christmas
03

Of Fire,
Wind &
Spirit

Of Fire, Wind & Spirit

by
James G. Littlepage

Published by
Jim's Poetry

Edited by T. A. Cole

Printed by Thomson-Shore, Inc. • Dexter, Michigan • 2003

First Edition
Published by Jim's Poetry in 2003
82086 Cow Creek Road, Seaside, OR, 97318

Printed in the United States of America
Printed by Thomson-Shore, Inc., Dexter, Michigan

Library of Congress Preassigned Card Number

ISBN 0-9745041-0-6 (Hardcover)
ISBN 0-9745041-1-4 (Paperback)

Cover: An Arizona sunset in August 2002 during the Rodeo-Chediski
fire provided by U.S. Forest Service firefighter Steve Palmer.

Dedication

I wish to dedicate this book to the memory of my grandfathers, Grandpa Littlepage who shared his poetry with me when I was very young and Grandpa Wallace who shared his imagination through his tall tales, and:

To Mrs. Dennison, my high school humanities teacher who challenged me to write "because you have a special talent". She affirmed, "I will give you an 'A' as your grade, but you must earn it by writing poetry." Thank you to "Mrs. D" for her encouragement.

To my mother, father, and my eleven siblings who listened to my poetry and encouraged me to continue. Throughout my life, they were my sounding board and my critics.

To my brother firefighters, my friends, and those individuals in passing who listened as I shared my poetry along life's way. Thank you for your unbridled responses and words of encouragement.

To my sons Jesse, who is here, and James, in heaven, both have made me very proud to be their father. The loss of James gives me a better understanding of God's gift of life to us through the death of His Son.

To my grandchildren Alyscia and Carson who give me great joy through the reality and truth that their love is unconditional. I know the circle of life is complete when I look at them.

And to Teresa, who God sent as an angel from my past (my high school prom date) to gather the scraps of paper, napkins, envelopes, and my memory to form *Of Fire, Wind & Spirit*. Without God's guidance and her input and hard work, this book would still be a box of paper.

Table of Contents

Preface

From an early age in my life, I felt the need to put on paper the words singing within my heart. Poetry is as much a part of who I am as the remaining hair on my head. I see, hear, touch, taste, and smell the beautiful tapestry of life and want to share all that I enjoy with others.

Acknowledgments

I wish to give special thanks to my friends and U.S. Forest Service firefighters Steve and Judy Palmer for providing the beautiful Arizona sunset photo taken near Heber/Overgaard during the Rodeo-Chediski fire in August of 2002 which graces the cover of this book. Steve's talented son Adam, professionally known as Cuhat, provided the humorous illustration that accompanies the poem *Day to Day Dreams*.

Introduction

Of Fire, Wind & Spirit is a collection of poems intended to create special moments for the reader. The section titled "Praises" presents the author's exaltation to God as well as a Christian message to the reader. The section titled "Along the Path" tracks the author from a ten-year old schoolboy to the present, forty years later, and essentially presents a biography in verse capturing the emotional depths of life's paths.

From cover to cover, the poems in each of the seven sections will allow the reader to experience a heightened emotional awareness, cross the Rocky Mountains, understand the loss of a son, love from the depths of the heart, feel the hot heat of fire, shout praises to God, lounge in daydreams, and simply watch the pendulum swing.

Though life takes us down many roads, it is the author's belief that it is the choices we make that determine our destination, and it is his expressed hope and desire that he meet each reader of this book someday in heaven.

Praises

The Unknown Soldier

I once was a soldier
with a man-killer in my hand
until one day a bullet struck me;
my blood ran in the sand.

Then darkness crept upon me,
and death was growing near.
It was then I heard the voice of Jesus;
it vanished all my fear.

He spoke with a voice of kindness,
embedded in His eyes, a true love.
He told me of a place called heaven,
a paradise, somewhere in the sky above.

Then He lifted my body
from the blood drenched sand;
He took away my rifle
and placed a Bible in my hand.

My Potter's Wheel

An undetermined future -
life's so unclear.
Today in the hands of the Potter,
I am only the clay.

Shape me
into a vessel of perfection.
Mold and caress my heart;
give me direction.

Study my recipe;
extract the times that bring a smile.
Mix them with desire,
then knead them for awhile.

Put me on the wheel
and gently throw this clay.
Turning slowly, the soft touch of my Potter's hand
shapes me in His way.

With no direction, dreams, or desire,
life has no meaning today.
Without the hands of the Potter,
I remain a block of clay.

I Believe

In darkness I called out and
God heard my cry.
I prayed for someone
to brighten my sky.

He said, "Do you believe?"
and said, "I do."
How amazing His grace;
I waited; He sent you.

He knew before our conception
what our destiny would be.
He filled our hearts with love,
then waited for my plea.

On that special day,
He lit up the stage.
He brought us together,
a new chapter, a new page.

As we touched,
I felt His warm embrace.
And through your smile,
I saw His loving face.

I sense life's joy
growing stronger with each day
as we share our lives
following His ways.

Each day will be much brighter
than the day before.
The light of love will shine forever,
and darkness will be no more.

A Psalm

Praise the Lord for His counsel in life's way as I walk
and for the satisfaction He gives when we talk.

He gives me tools for the choices I am to make;
He steadies my feet upon the path I am to take.

He maps out my journey; His direction I seek.
He takes my hand and leads me in times when I am weak.

In despair, He sustains, but in love and faith, He amplifies.
The Comforter is with me; His glory magnifies.

He sent Jesus as my Savior; I know the Son of Man.
He suffers all things to pass according to his plan.

I rejoice in this knowledge; He is waiting on the other side
with loving arms to greet me; in Him, I will abide.

The Eye of the Maker

The eye of the Maker
sees the path that I choose.
His direction, His Word,
I follow or loose.

My prayer,
to gain the wisdom I seek.
My heritage, Indian Irish;
it's hard to be meek.

I understand the message
and try to comply.
A life of adventure and freedom
but someday to die.

In hopes that my testimony
will withstand the test,
my name in the Book
with all of the blessed.

The path I choose
will give me my stay.
When I meet my Maker,
somewhere - someday.

When You're Down

"Place your hand in mine;
let me lead you for a while.
Travel with me on life's journey;
I'll give you a smile.

"I'll lead you through the valley,
a place to rest by a quiet stream,
across the rocky mountains,
a place where you can dream."

If you take the time to listen
and you kneel to pray,
words of comfort and of joy
you will hear Him say.

"Believe in me, that is all I ask.
And you shall know of My great love.
Open up your heart and mind;
there is a place for you above."

Destination

In the darkness of winter's night or on a bright summer's day,
He shall be my guiding light to help me find my way.
A way unknown to all, or so it seems to be,
for no one really knows what life holds for me.

One thing that is certain, this, to you I say,
all men must have a purpose; I've found mine today.
The service of my Lord, in every way I know,
makes my guided light to shine its magnificent glow.

Lighting the way along life's unpaved road,
giving me the strength, to carry my heavy load.
That is all good for me, you say, but what about you?
Give your heart to God; He'll tell you what to do.

Someday we shall all meet
to join hand in hand,
as our light shines through the gate
to God's promise land.

Our Compass

The scope of life is overwhelming,
but the Word, our compass, points the way.
Traveling within the circle of life,
we live from day to day.

What hope is there
except for another tomorrow?
When does the joy begin
from this circle of sorrow?

Peace lives within;
the scriptures say it's true.
Our direction, we find, is through Jesus;
then, what are we to do?

We believe in Him.
But the world says, "That's a lie!
Live today for yourself
for tomorrow you shall die."

Follow the compass, our Great Counselor, the Alpha and Omega,
He guides us; He leads us; He carries us, too.
He'll be there with us
when this life is through.

God Reigns

The words "I do"
are but a seed
to be cultivated with love
in word, in thought, in deed.

To be nurtured with kindness
in all manners of caring,
the fruits of this bond
will then be worth sharing.

A great fortress is marriage
for all to acknowledge and see
as a tiny seed grows
into a mighty tree.

Able to withstand all that comes
in times of good and times of bad,
living on strength, then on roots
when times are sad.

Bearing your burdens on limbs of love
within His hands so secure
as He is the Maker of all seeds;
with His love you can endure.

Though many seeds may be planted,
without His love they cannot grow.
Today this challenge is for two;
will you, as one, make this so?

When you share the fruit
from those limbs of love
and receive His blessings,
He reigns from above.

Enriching the lives
of all those around,
good wishes on your journey together;
God speed, you're heaven bound.

His Gifts

A daily quiet time,
to ponder the gifts we take for granted.
Not a bad thought,
this seed You've planted.

The gift of life
and time to share,
a helping hand
to show I care.

A blue bird's song;
its message is clear.
In my thoughts,
You're always near.

The Trail of Life

On a mountain trail high above the river,
you will find me riding there.
To reach the summit is my goal,
though I know not when nor where.

The only light visible,
sparks, when rocks and horseshoes meet.
The assurance, though unseen,
there's still ground beneath my horse's feet.

Each step takes me closer as I slide
through the thick black air
to reach the comfort of my camp,
somewhere way up there.

"Should I stop?" my mind proposes;
though unspoken, the question is there.
The answer is slow in coming
for my eyes cannot see where.

I travel on by faith,
maybe on the trail, who knows? It's night.
What is that leaking through the fog?
I think per chance it's light.

Breaking out of the dreary darkness
into an artist's picture of perfection,
this land sculptured by God
without man's correction,

My horse stops, sensing my desire
to etch this rare moment of beauty into my mind.
Never before and probably never again as a mortal
will I see beauty of this kind.

A large florescent moon sends shafts of light
to dance upon the mountain's head.
A sea of fog as white as snow
makes up the mountain's feather bed.

As I sit in admiration of this beauty
God made for me,
I realize He brought me through the darkness;
how important I must be.

Conquering Death

Now arise and look up;
there may be a tear in your eye.
It's great to know that you can go
with your head held high.

Know that God forgives,
and know that we are all sinners.
Death can be conquered;
if I believe; if I repent.

We'll Play in Heaven

God said, "I will lead you.
Come and take my hand.
We'll run and play together
in the promise land."

"You will meet some old friends
and see your family, too,
but first I must tell you,
your work there is not through.

"Time to get on with living;
go and make amends.
People do not understand, but
I do, and I forgive your sins."

"God, there is one thing I need
that only you can give;
I need to see the book of life
before I can live."

"I know you put others first," He said,
"That's a good trait, you know.
The names you seek are in the book,
because I love them so."

As tears of joy began to fall,
I said "What can I do?"
He said, "Be still and listen;
your work there is not through.

"Satan has been testing you
to see how much you'd take.
I allowed it all to happen;
I knew you wouldn't break.

14

"But because you are human
and all are prone to sin,
ask for forgiveness daily
so Satan can't get in.

"Most of all, in all things,
show others My great love,
so they can visualize their place
in My heaven up above.

"One day I will come;
so hold these things to be true.
We will laugh and play in heaven
with friends and family too."

Heaven

To say hello
and never say good-by,
to wear a smile
and never cry,
to live in truth
and never lie,
to live in peace
and never die.

The Race

A man in his life
must do many things to survive.
His word must be gold,
his spirit, creative and alive.

Self-esteem from his Maker
and dignity from within.
The ability to accept
the loss or the win.

He must live, give love, and
focus little on worldly stuff,
live his life for others,
help when things are tough.

Be a friend to all,
realize their need.
The fruit of love
comes from but a seed.

Have faith like a mountain;
rise above all that you see.
The Lord is a friend
for you and me.

Then, too, we must realize
that in this pace,
we have to help others
that fall from the race.

It's not whether you lose or place,
and even if you do,
it's how you ran the race
when this life is through.

When these days are over
and all is said and done,
He'll be there to greet you,
"You ran a good race, my son."

Slow Down

God, I'm sure, sent me as a blessing, so slow down.
No, stop, and take my hand.
He made all of this for you and I. Join me and
inhale the fragrance of our land.

His work - the Earth, the heavens, and everything,
perfectly fashioned in all ways.
He gave us life, not as a challenge, but as a gift.
He gave us breath, but numbered our days.

Take His gift and the time we have and smile,
for His blessing and His love
are God's way of telling you He's watching
from His throne high above.

And when your journey takes you to the promise land,
He'll say, "Slow down, no, stop, and take my hand.
I sent you a dove
to let you know life is based on love."

Days

Numbered are the days
set on this earth.
Parents are chosen
even before one's birth.

Many tasks to complete,
many stages of life.

Times ever changing,
trouble and strife.

Acceptance of our journey,
choices, situations.
The way we face judgment
at the end of trials and tribulations.

Will we choose an eye for an eye
or turn the other cheek?
Will we choose to show our strength
or to be silent and meek?

The Shield, God's Word,
we must know it and use it
so that in the game of life,
we are prepared to loose.

But in this life, a loss
could really be a win,
if we know the Savior
and choose to invite Him in.

Remember our days are numbered,
and we must not wait too long.
When the roll is called up yonder,
what a wonderful song.

So walk through life's stages with God;
reflect His goodness in all that you do.
The days will not be numbered in heaven
when this life is through.

A Crown of Thorns

Traveling through the mountains of northern Arkansas,
there's a treasure to be discovered.
Off the beaten path, up the hill, along the rock wall,
there among the dogwoods and redbuds, a majestic structure.

Built of glass and wood, a place of worship,
simple yet complex.
The diamonds of glass are as we are in our walk.
The pillar of strength, He holds us up.

Stand on the outside, gaze through the glass,
Thorncrown Chapel lies within.
Enter and feel the presence of God;
pray; hold hands with a friend.

Loosen all within your heart;
make it transparent; let Him see its end.
The forgiving heart of God will greet you;
He can cleanse you from your sin.

Accept His invitation; you can see more clearly than before.
Life's barriers turn effervescent like the panes of Thorncrown.
His Word will lead you; His hands will guide you;
His strength will be yours; His majesty will never let you down.

Do you know the Son who died wearing a crown of thorns
with tears in His eyes on the cross at Calvary?
His tears were for you; then, He arose.
Repent; ask Jesus into your heart; He will set you free.

Thorncrown Chapel, only a symbol of His crown of thorns.
Death represents the day you will be free.
Life is everlasting because He bore sin's misery on the cross.
Thank you, Jesus, for suffering for me at Calvary.

The Comforter

When this life is over
and mine has just begun,
I'll be there with my Savior;
He is God's only Son.

He came to earth so long ago
to give his life for me.
Pure at heart and with a gentle spirit,
He died to set me free.

He never leaves us all alone;
He's the Comforter, you see.
He walks and talks and shadows us
wherever we're to be.

He guards us from all danger
and corrects us when we're bad.
He's there when we pray
and cries when we are sad.

He'll guide us through this life
in all we have to do.
Then we'll be there with Him in heaven
when this life is completely through.

Jesus Loves Me

Jesus loves me,
but it's hard for me to see.
God's grace is greater
than all my sins could be.

Jesus said, "I am here.
I want to walk with you."
Though I cannot believe He wants to
after all I've put him through.

There were times I didn't love Him,
and times I didn't care.
But every time I turned around,
my Jesus was still there.

He said, "I gave my life for you
so that your life would never end."
When you choose everlasting life,
you let the Savior in.

He'll take away your sadness;
it's such a great joy, you'll cry.
He'll let you visualize the place
He has for you on high.

He'll take your hand and lead you
if you ask Him to.
The trials and fires of this life,
He will see you through.

When your days on Earth are over,
there is one thing that I know.
You'll be there with Him in heaven;
the Bible tells me so.

Choices

Traveling the roads of life, we cover countless miles
enduring many hardships and facing all of life's trials.
If we stop and dwell on all the things we've lost,
we do not smell the flowers because we fear the cost.

If we fail to enter the race thinking we cannot win,
we'll stand beside the road and watch; we'll never enter in.
Our life will be void of meaning; we'll know not who we are;
our head we'll hang in self pity; we'll miss His shining star.

Alas! Just stop and listen. Don't you hear the angels cry?
We travel too fast this road of life; they weep for you and I.
Take the time to seek His Majesty on high;
with all the love He has for us, we do not have to die.

Have faith and give glory to the King.
Stop and smell the roses and hear the angels sing.
Your choices will determine your road. Death waits around the bend.
We all start out together, but only you can choose the end.

The End

The Earth will split;
mountains will fall.
God will be here
to judge one and all.

It may be today,
tomorrow, or next year.
But people will call
and tremble with fear.

They'll all be down
on bended leg.
They'll pray, they'll cry,
for mercy they'll beg.

The unrighteous, the wicked,
the unbeliever, the bad.
All at this time will suffer;
it's really so sad.

For if they had not chosen
to go the wrong way,
they could rejoice
on God's judgment day.

Along the Path

Grandpa Taught Me

As I look back to the days of my youth,
I think of Grandpa Rufus, the time we shared, the joy.
I remember a special day, one that helped to shape my life
though unknown at the time to a ten-year old boy.

I watched as he fed and groomed his team of horses
to prepare them for the task at hand.
Methodically, he harnessed and hooked them to the plow;
he put the reins across his back - time to plow the land.

I walked or ran along beside him as he worked.
Sweat trickled across his brow; he always had a smile.
Feeling his strength in me and bold because he was,
I asked, "Grandpa, could I plow for a while?"

He stopped and looked me in the eye,
"I believe you can," he said. Grandpa trusted me.
Over the old oak plow handles,
I could barely see.

"Ha" for right and "gee" for left,
the horses understand.
He put the reins across my back;
that day, I plowed the land.

Grandpa taught me how to plow that day.
I noted his attitude, his preparation, and his team;
through his love, trust, and understanding,
he taught me how to build a dream.   Thank you, Grandpa.

Grandma

Southern cooking and southern hospitality,
Clementine's kitchen, Grandma to me.
She made homemade cornbread, red beans and ham,
buttermilk biscuits, and strawberry jam.

Rufus had a little round belly, Grandpa of mine;
he loved the cooking of Grandma Clementine.
Of Rufus and Clemmie, my memories last;
I miss them both, the south, my past.

Dad

Dad was a tough man,
a good father and to many a friend.
I remember him a giant from my youth
who shaped my beginning, my destiny's end.

Honesty, a man's word, is his bond.
Be who you are, no pretenses.
Be open, live your dreams,
build relationships not fences.

Always give your very best in everything you do.
Never quit a job you start until that job is through.
There is nothing you can't accomplish, if you will it so,
said the man who shaped my life before he had to go.

Mom

In the morning light of Christmas day,
I see my childhood clearly now.
In the old house on the hill, a product of love,
I asked myself how.

Where did I come from, and why?
I see a gift, a baby's seed,
nurtured in my mothers womb;
what a noble deed.

You and dad gave me life,
and because of that, I am blessed.
From my first heartbeat in this life,
you gave me the very best.

With love and understanding,
you taught me all the rules.
You filled my heart with goodness,
and now my hands are tools.

A servant of God, of humanity,
and of the land of my birth.
All because you loved me
and built within my worth.

When I was bad, I'd hear your voice,
"You're a good boy," you would say.
Though I wasn't, your words made me grow
into the man I am today.

Thank you, mom, my teacher and my friend;
I think of you each day.
Even now, as your great grandchildren beckon,
you taught me the very best way.

My Quill

I do not know why
I have been chosen to write.
The depth of emotion takes it's toll.
Shall I sleep tonight?

My mind races as blood flows
hot from within.
My heart pounds out a message
transferred to my pen.

I write a script
from the depths of my soul,
seeking God's favor
in truth to be whole.

Writing to tell a story
as I travel toward home,
He travels with me;
I am not alone.

I write of love,
of passion, and of pain.
I write by the fireplace
or out in the rain.

I write for His message
sent from above.
The fruit of the Spirit
is God's love.

My life in poetry,
as I dip my quill,
seeking everlasting life,
His blood is my seal.

The Belief of a Man

Today I am full
of grief and of sorrow
with a thought of life
and a fear of tomorrow.

For tomorrow in Viet Nam, I will be
in a land of war stricken with hate.
I tell you this now, I'm alive;
for tomorrow, it may be too late.

But even if death comes
to me and to many more,
it will not be in vain
because this you would even die for.

We fight for freedom, our families,
America, and a land without war.
Millions of people have died,
and there will be millions more.

Because there are many people
who do not think as I,
this is why there is war
and why people will continue to die.

Arrow

Arrow, my trusted steed,
we've traveled many miles together,
many lonely mountain trails
in all kinds of weather.

I remember when I found you;
you were just three years old,
headed for the slaughter house.
Too wild to break, I was told.

The strength you possessed,
those wild mustang eyes,
calmed by a greenhorn's touch
much to everyone's surprise.

You gave the little children rides,
and to all you gave great joy.
But most of all your servitude,
to my once little boy.

You saved me from the river,
two times from freezing rain and cold.
No greater bond or friendship,
so know you'll never be sold.

Only death, when it comes,
will part our ways.
For we have many more miles
to travel in the coming days.

And as we travel those miles together,
I thank you, my old friend.
No greater horse has ever lived,
your spirit is the wind.

Father's Duty

You wanted
more than I could give.
Forget that I am;
go on with life and live.

I wanted you - I needed you
so I could be strong.
Tormented today and tomorrow for sure,
but, alas, I found my thoughts were wrong.

Seeking my inner self,
not knowing how.
Loving a certainty,
not sure now.

Complex equation,
two into one.
Life long commitment,
father to son.

Separation's a reality;
new life is freed.
Your friendship forever,
a blessing to me.

Diane's Bouquet

Through the melting snow,
a chill yet in the air,
a tiny weed pushed through the rocky ground
into the world without a care.

The weed fought for every breath,
enduring endless trials to survive.
As time went on and roots put down,
the world would know she was alive.

The sun moved north, she bathed in warmth,
stretched out her leaves up to the sky.
Through hurricanes and thunder storms
she held on, her mission not to die.

To flower on this rocky ledge,
a place she called home.
To raise three bulbs and have
them planted deep into sandy loam.

As days passed, a bud appeared;
He provided sunshine and mid-day showers.
Some watched in awe as this little weed
transformed into a flower.

A thing of beauty, her offspring felt
her warmth and nurturing way.
She gave them everything to grow,
protected them day by day.

Not knowing when her time would be up,
she chose with them to stay
until the day His hand came down;
time to go away.

From heaven's bouquet where she now resides,
He'll send the fragrance of her love.
Watching as her children grow,
from her perch up high above.

My children, someday you will understand
why God's hand took her away.
I choose to remember her smile as she looked at you.
Children, you were Diane's bouquet.

The Last Dance

Are you wondering what will it take
for me to get a clue?
I don't know, but if you continue,
someday I'll take the cue.

I should be able to understand
you don't really care for me.
But love is blind, and I love you;
therefore, I cannot see.

In my mind's eye, I see the good times;
we shared our life.
I see our wedding day with smiles and happiness;
we loved, we said, "I do," as husband and wife.

I see dancing, touching, holding, and caring;
I remember times of great joy -
December 14, in the afternoon,
with the birth of our little boy.

I see our children growing up,
Sports, birthdays, togetherness, what a time we had.
There were times when all was not good,
times together when we were sad.

Through thick and thin, good and bad,
and great, or not the best,
we had one thing, our true love.
Time after time, it stood the test.

But this true love is one-sided now
without hope, prayer, or a chance.
If you give this old fool his due
and on this New Year's his last dance,

Then, he'll always remember you with a smile
and hope your dreams come true.
You can remember me as an old fool
who finally took his cue.

Green's Farm

God's angels, they await you,
your company they seek,
here now to keep away the demons
and give you restful sleep.

White garments, wings and halos,
warm smiles, filled with love;
God's angels, they await you
for your journey up above.

They'll each take your hand and lead you;
all three will fly away
to make your place in heaven,
and await our coming day.

You've always been here for us,
but your work on Earth is complete.
It's time to rise above
to take your glory seat.

Your parents, brothers, sons, and grandson,
even your friends are waiting there.
Their eyes above the clouds,
they wait for you up there.

With shouts of joy and jubilation
as they see ole Green arrive,
they'll proclaim through celebration;
you'll know that God's alive.

He'll take your hand and lead you,
along with all your clan.
He'll smile and then embrace you,
"Here is your farm, young man."

It's then you'll realize,
by past study, you'll understand;
the Bible, God's Word, is true;
there is a promise land.

I'll Be Waiting Because I Love You

There are many Jameses here, Jesus,
but I have just arrived.
I need your help; I left so quickly
and didn't have a chance to say good-bye.

To all my friends and loved ones
and to those my life I shared,
I need to get a message
to all for whom I cared.

I didn't mean to leave so quickly,
but God needed me, you see,
to build with Him and Jesus
a place for you and me.

So don't be sad; keep me with you
in spirit, mind, and heart.
Know that if there were a choice,
I'd have chosen to not depart.

But God made the choice for me;
He wanted me to go.
He needed me to be here with Him
just so you'd know.

In this place called heaven;
I'll be waiting here for you.
I'll show you how to hunt and fish here
and all the other things to do.

We'll walk across the meadows,
hand in hand, our dreams to share.
Until then, do not forget me,
because for you I really care.
Bye, Dad. Love, James.

The Day My Spirit Died

Memories of a distant past,
a smile filled each day.
Lost one day in time,
the joy slipped away.

I remember being fulfilled
and in all things content
until my heart moved away.
The void it left, for rent.

Many people checked it out,
but none allowed me to stay.
Some lingered for a while,
those I chased away.

No one could understand
what went on inside.
My James left this world,
the day my spirit died.

That day, I saw my son
lying in a casket bed.
Tears and cries of anguish,
I wished I were dead.

Had it not been for my other son Jess,
I would have left also.
A bond as strong as steel,
his love wouldn't let me go.

It's been a long time now
and time heals; I still protect his space.
But Jess's love works overtime
to keep me in my place.

My smile is now returning,
only through God's grace.
Jess lives with me here on earth,
but in the heavens, I see James' face.

Their spirit lies within my chest,
and I can say, "All is well."
Don't cross my path against them
for I have been to hell.

Tough Times

We had a few rough times
as fathers and sons always do.
Son James and Dad are gone now.

Thank you, son Jess,
for your strength, your mind, and your heart.
You made the very best of all these attributes
from the very start.

At this time I need to draw emotional support
from all you have within
as I start my life alone;
it's hard to begin again.

Because you've always been there,
and I know you always will be.
To God I give all the praise
for your love and what you mean to me.

And for our future as it comes,
things we've yet to share.
In joy and in times of need,
I promise I'll always be there.

Time Heals

Time heals, they say,
but it takes away our youth.
Today is a pleasant day;
I feel my angel near.

Thoughts of father and of son, both were Jameses, as am I.
I am here, and they have gone away.
Their deeds must have been complete,
I don't know why, but I will someday.

When we meet again,
I will most certainly show them my love's embrace.
James, my son, I would have given all for you
had I been allowed to take your place.

But all things are as they should be
whether or not I agree.
I'll smile, make the most of life,
for God knows what's best for me.

Then someday, the James trio will be united,
the past and future as one.
My father, his father, and me
will all be together with our son.

Life is grand, so live each day
as if your last; know that it could be.
Then we will pass with no regrets;
what does the future hold for thee?

Alyscia

A pretty little baby, a bright and shining star.
Brought into this world per chance an angel from afar.

I can see the halo, grandfathers can you know.
Planning for her future as I watch this angel grow.

Glasses off my nose, hat on the floor,
hat back on, she smiles; time to play some more.

Irish heritage passed on through the daughter of my son.
If all the world were Irish, life would be more fun.

I pray for her happiness, her health, and safety too.
I pray in times of danger God will see her through.

I pray that she will sustain life's grueling test.
God and grandpa's angel will be the very best.

Cradled next to mom and dad, so snugly to God's chest,
Grandpa knows that his angel has been blessed.

Fire Triangles

The Fireman's Watch

We sped down the lane hurrying with lights and sirens.
Flames from the window, "I just went to the mailbox," she cried.
"Please save my baby. He's inside."
I kicked and burst through the door, but all life was consumed.
That day my first baby died, and later, a fireman cried.

"A child through the ceiling," came the call.
I prayed all would be well;
but the six year old life left Earth that day.
We tried to revive him but to no avail.
Late that night, a fireman cried.

Behind the badge lies a soft, tender heart;
without this shield, we always feel the pain.
In times of new grief, we question our actions and skill.
To gain an edge or achieve perfection, we study, we train.
You may think we are invincible, or are we insane?

We challenge fire,
storms, and tragedy.
On public assists,
we come
whenever you call.

The chief broadcasts the first response,
"Fire attack, your report?"
"Fully involved interior, intense heat,
heavy flames in the hall!"
"Making progress, the fire is contained."

But the outstretched lifeless hands, I still recall.
"Lieutenant," he said, "A body count."
"Eight, most children," the lieutenant replied.
Today the watch ended, each hope had died;
then much later, a fireman cried.

Fire Fighter Soldiers of Rodeo-Chediski

Marching in groups, tools in hand,
trucks and dozers across the land.
Birds and planes fill the sky,
today's the day, fire, time to die.

Command group here, plans are made,
support is ready, the tracks are laid.
Take it to the enemy in the devil's hand,
all are ready to protect this land.

All working as a team hand to hand,
our mission to protect America's land.
Our goal to battle this manmade hell,
all to succeed, our story to tell.

Blazing trees, smoke filled sky,
take it to the devil, time to die.
At the day's end, you will pass the test;
God is with you; you will be blessed.

The American Breed

Three hundred and forty-three brothers and sisters died
the day the towers fell.
They gave their lives for others;
no one went to hell.

Greater love hath no man
than to give his life for another.
When you call for help,
expect no less than a brother.

We all belong to the same clan;
we love you; we are your brother.
Expect no less than our best,
for America is our mother.

We are "the American Breed,"
we accept that as our creed.
To die in the line of duty,
to save you, it's our deed.

For when you are in trouble,
our life is blessed.
We strive to save you
for it is our quest.

We train; we challenge;
we keep physically fit; we test.
We give you our youth, our strength, and our knowledge -
always our very best.

We do not dwell on those we've lost.
We send them home with bagpipes, singing "Amazing Grace."
Their angels, then, watch over us
as we smile and stare danger in the face.

Brothers and sisters of
the American breed, our clan,
we strive to beat the pace.
But per chance we fall, it's His plan;

Let tears stream down your face.
It's okay to cry; just remember,
we are protected by His grace.
We will give our lives for you;
in heaven, you will see our face.

911

The towers fell
and firemen died.
You'll recall
America cried.

Albuquerque Fire Camp

As I lie here listening to the night sounds of fire camp,
my thoughts drift to the young juveniles - I wonder if they knew.
The sparks from their fireworks turned to flames; smoke filled the sky.
A 911 call, dispatch the crew!

More than initial attack can handle,
the wind driven flames are in a flurry.
Faster beats the public's heart;
their cry, "Please help, and hurry!"

The drums send out a message
to notify the team.
The knights prepare to battle the dragon;
the media sends out a scream.

The team arrives; plans are made.
Safety – always number one.
The sun is red; smoke plumes blacken the sky;
the dragon makes a run.

My throat is raspy from the smoky air;
my nostrils burn.
Yet the wind drifts my way,
and I smell breakfast.

Albuquerque Fire Camp is alive this morning,
showers and laundry, a store,
the four star restaurant, and our "city hall";
all built in one day.

Showered and fed, we all meet
to hear the incident action plan, the IAP.
What will it take to kill the dragon?
What is expected of me?

Planning, logistics, operations, and finance,
we are the fire fighting team - always our best.
The Montaño and the Atrisco fires are out,
and once again we've stood the test.

Toboggan Run

He lit up the forest
with high voltage grounded by a tree;
it commanded our attention.
"To Idaho," summoned the dispatcher's plea.

"Fire in the pan-handle forest,
the mountain above Toboggan River Run."
Named by a scholar from the past,
a rapid winding decent from the sun.

The fire serpent coiled and reared its finely chiseled head
to deliver a fiery strike to this sculptured land.
The Gray team arrived, a meeting, a plan,
consensus, "We're going to need a hand."

"Logistics, make it happen; set the stage.
Get everyone here right away."
For when the curtain rises,
our team, poised and ready, we can safely play.

Shafts of flaming carbon formed from the serpent's mouth;
a western run sets more hills ablaze.
The snag patch on fire, tumbling debris,
safety, a question in this forest maze.

Somewhere a prayer received,
delivered by the wind to the Artist of the sky.
The contents I do not know,
But in essence, "Dear Lord, please help," the cry.

He hears all; the plea fits His plan.
A divine air drop directed by His hand.
Still so much more to do
for we are but caretakers of His land.

Not quite as quickly as it started,
we'll finish here and be on our way
waiting for the dispatcher's call as we rest
to battle the serpent, another place, another day.

Fire! Fire!

Fire! Fire! The lady in red cried.
The curly haired fireman took his hose line inside.

Smoke from the windows, flames from the door,
his first taste of fire, and he wanted no more.

The lady in red, he made her his wife.
This curly haired fireman, his first taste of life.

Fire! Fire! The lady in blue cried.
The curly haired fireman took his hose line inside.

Motorcycles and racing, a part of his life,
the lady in blue, now Randy's new wife.

Fire! Fire! Cried the lady in brown.
So goes the short story in our little town.

Mr. Lucky they called him in all of his fame,
his struggle in life for fraulein and flame.

Oh, curly haired fireman, it's time to step down
from a career long commitment, the best job around.

Fire! Fire! Cried the lady with hair of gold.
The curly haired fireman on life, now was sold.

A life long commitment to the lady of gold.
No more fires to fight, just have fun growing old.

Rog's Career

Follow the leader, Roger played it well.
Childhood to manhood - no one could tell.
Toy trucks to fire trucks, old trucks and new,
the "A" shift troop, they were his crew.

Drive fast to calls;
the cat's in a tree.
"Cut the rope now, boys,"
kitty be free.

"Keep the trucks clean boys," Rog would say,
"Drive 'em fast."
"First to the call, boys;
don't ever be last."

The strike team leader,
fought fire on the fly,
slipped in the shower,
heck of a guy.

Don't worry, Deb;
he'll be home all day.
We'll all come over to see
if Rog can play.

Gaston to Montana,
a dream not true.
Fire chief of Gaston,
is in store for you.

Time to leave now, Rog.
Thanks and good luck.
Wish you could be ridin' with us
in our brand new truck.

Your heart as the power,
your grit made it go.
And, oh, not to worry,
we won't drive it slow.

Fireman Jim

Bouncing down Farmington Road
in my '73 Ford truck,
the potholes, there for a role,
I don't believe in luck.

I must be on time to begin
the meeting of Local 2210.
But a stranded motorist I see;
I'll help and be on my way again.

"Hello, madam; I see you have a flat.
I'd be glad to give you assistance today."
"It's okay, sir," she said.
"Help is on the way."

I turned and walked away.
"Fireman Jim!" the toddler proclaimed.
"Oh, please, sir," the lady spoke. "Are you a fireman?
Is Jim really your name?"

"Yes, ma'am; I taught your son
emergency 911 in his daycare class.
'I'm Fireman Jim,' I tell the kids.
Your son's a smart young lad."

"Can you help us?" she said.
"No one's really coming; I'm all alone today."
I changed the tire, gave Jake a badge,
then went on about my way.

The union members waited;
I knew they would.
When I said I'd fixed a flat,
each one there understood.

A Firefighter Reflects

I do solemnly swear . . . hallowed be thy name . . .
and to the republic for which it stands . . .
purple mountains' majesty . . . America, America . . . commitment . . .
July for freedom, September for labor, February for love, April for hope.
Some have journeyed on . . . Father, Son, Friends and all.
We shall follow.
Look ahead . . . Look back . . . Where to?. . . It's certain . . . Your choice.
We seek to climb the highest mountain.
I'm in charge! Be a servant. Build a team.
Respect His authority. Frown on self-made authority.
Follow your heart . . . Build a dream . . . for life . . . your dream.
Take time to love and let others love you.
Enjoy your travels and journey for you may never reach your destination,
but finish if you can.
Promise to tell the truth . . . and nothing but the truth so help you God . . .
One nation under God . . . God shed His grace on thee . . .
Calendar year . . . New Year . . . Hope . . .
Independence . . . brotherhood.
Our duty to quench the raging flames, until death do us part.
Hope to see you later. Until then . . . happy trails.

Reflections on Love

First Kiss

My darling, I must tell you
I am a man
who has sought love
throughout life.

I have given freely of myself
to those with needs and desires,
seeking little in return,
nonetheless a happy man.

For I knew, somewhere
I would meet the person that was made for me
and I for her.
You are that person.

I knew from the moment
of our first kiss
that the bonds of love were tied
never to be broken.

I know that I am but a man, nothing more,
and all that I am belongs to you.
In my dreams, you are my hope,
my inspiration, and my destiny.

Oh! To become reality someday.
On the other hand, I realize
because I dream of love in life
that does not make it so.

But through this kiss we shared,
I sensed you felt it, too.
You opened up your heart
and made my dream come true.

Please let me know
if this feeling was amiss.
I'd die a little but with a smile.
I'll remember that first kiss.

No More Shadows

The fire dancing on the logs in the fireplace, though beautiful and bright,
casts shadows that were not there before.
And there as I gaze into the flame of life
I wonder but cannot see the shadows.

I know they are there
for at times they covered the light of my life.
You are that light.
As my fire burns, I will not fall again into the shadows.

Rise above the darkness and take his hand.
For guidance and direction, He will provide
in this life and forever and
as long as there is a flame.

In this life, I will look to you
to quench the fire that burns within.

All I Have

My love sleeps with you each night
and shadows you each day
to protect you from harm. He stands guard
in hopes to keep the demons away.

Though he is strong, he can be broken by you.
Nothing can distract him from his duty.
But if you do not want my love,
please send him home; he is all I have.

Your Huckleberry

I'll be your huckleberry,
and you can be my vine.
Love will have no measure
as our lives entwine.

But if you choose another -
this obligation that you carry,
cut me from the vine,
I'll be no one's huckleberry.

Journey into Darkness

I do not wish to be
ten years older,
but if that is what it will take,
I wish I were.

But if I were ten years wiser,
I may wish to be ten years younger.
For every moment we're apart,
seems to last forever.

And every moment we are
together seems to quickly slip away.
Only through the memories
do those fleeting times stay alive.

Because I have a vivid picture
of your laughter and smile, I see
the twinkle in your eyes
as you look as me.

I will wait for ten years
or for an eternity
just to share one moment of
a lifetime with you.

Visions

Walking through the winter darkness,
a chill yet in the air.
Visions of a lady
with beauty quite rare.

A proud lioness
in control of her lair.
Visions of a lady,
she seems without a care.

I sense deep emotion;
a desire to love is there.
Visions of a lady,
a life is but to share.

A guarded heart I see
from pain, I know not where.
Visions of a lady,
you with coal black hair.

Stroll with me, my friend,
through the winter air.
Visions of you, lady,
this night is ours to share.

Love and Dreams Last Forever

It's okay to live in a dream world;
at least that's what I tell myself.

But when I awake, frustration sets in;
I'm destined to be a man in search of a dream.

Somewhere, love means more than life itself.
A dreamer can see that; yes, I can.

But it's just beyond my reach
seemingly never to be attained in this life.

However, I shall continue to freely give, seek, and dream
even until life ends.

Dreams

There was a time last week when I had dreams;
I thought they would come true.
I knew whatever came was okay
because you had me and I had you.

I dreamed we would be alone at last,
together in our place.
I dreamed of your smile
as I softly touched your face.

My dreams were fairly simple.
All I wanted was to be
a special part of your life
as you sat there next to me.

I dreamed of growing old together,
walking hand in hand.

I dreamed of holding you in my arms
by the ocean, in the sand.

I dreamed your love would flow like a river,
the current would sweep me away.
I dreamed you'd be there for me
each and every day.

Then you woke me up;
you said, "It's time to go.
I don't love you any more.
I thought that you should know."

The bad in me is gone;
the good will always be.
God has given me the strength
to face reality.

I didn't know there were
so many things to do;
I only wish that you could be there to love me
as much as I loved you.

Daydreams

My eye photographed the beauty stored within your heart.
I see your smile as I reflect whenever we're apart.

My dreams and life entwine; as I look up, I see your face.
All things are real with you and in their proper place.

At ease with life, your touch confirms my trust.
I believe our thoughts are shared of friendship and life, of love and lust.

God is in control; with Him, three is not a crowd.
Eternal life is a reality, a blue sky without a cloud.

Your warmth is my sunshine; your smile, a cool summer's breeze.
To hold your hand, to embrace, to linger, and appease.

My life is full of dreams; make my dreams come true.
Grant me a gift, my prayer, to share some time with you.

Contentment

I listened to your breath
as you slept peacefully upon my chest.
I saw clearly for the first time His majesty, the beauty of life;
I am blessed.

I saw your smile and listened to your laughter;
as we danced, I felt our hearts embrace.
I looked into your eyes and saw His love.
As an angel painted a masterpiece in my mind, I saw your face.

I inhaled your fragrance, and I touched you
experiencing all that life has to give.
I thank you for fulfilling my desire to know
life's true meaning, time to live.

I felt your chest rise and fall next to me.
Neither riches or fame could compare; I'm blessed.
With the knowledge that life's fulfillment for me is your love,
I closed my eyes to rest.

My Sweetheart

My sweetheart means more to me
than all and many things.
I see her in the future
in my fondest hopes and dreams.

As I sit and watch at midnight,
the blueness of the sky,
I see a vision of her face
while clouds pass slowly by.

Then I think of us together,
a tender kiss, a smile.
Just to sit and be near her
and linger for a while.

I would wait a lifetime
just to see that smile.
Then I would know throughout eternity
the waiting had been worthwhile.

Someday

Over the rainbow,
somewhere,
believe in me.
Know that I am there.

I'm a dreamer,
you must know by now.
All things are possible, I somehow
do believe.

We'll find the path
as we play.
Seeking together,
finding it some way.

Sharing blue skies and rainbows -
"Only good things," we'll say.
Life together,
someday.

Sweetheart Flowers

Reaching through time and space,
I touch the planet Jupiter as I gather this bouquet for you.
I look back at Mother Earth;
you're there, and dreams do come true.

Look to the northwest
above the horizon into the sky
next to Jupiter; there, not a star,
only your reflection in my eye.

May the petals of this relationship
bring a smile to your heart.
This day has new meaning
because it's a new start.

My Rose

I could say "I love you" with a flower, a rose;
I could write "I love you" with my pen, in prose.

I could project "I love you" with a smile, it shows;
I could tell the world "I love you", everyone knows.

I can not hide "I love you", it grows;
everywhere I go, my love for you goes.

For you are truly
my fragrance of life, my rose.

Why?

I say, "I love you."
and you ask me, "Why?"
Why do the mountains
reach for the sky?

Why do the rivers
flow to the sea?
Would there be honey
without the bee?

I love your touch, your smile, your warm embrace;
I love your hair, your eyes, the look on your sweet face.
What else could take your place?
You are my existence and surely my stay.

Army Days

Why is it now, oh, God
that I have to be away?
Suffering the pains and sadness of life,
my heart, so sad today.

Oh, someday I'll be with her
all sadness to an end.
Laying in a field of clover
listening to the wind.

My life would have a meaning
a future I could see.
Gone would be my heartbreaks;
how happy I would be.

Somewhere in the future
with her I want to be.
Someway, somehow I see it;
then sad, I'll never be.

Because someday God will see us
putting love into each heart.
From that day on we'll be together
never again to part.

Lifetime Love

Many tears I have cried
since I left you on that day
to go and serve my country
in a land so far away.

I remember leaving you,
your eyes so filled with tears.
You said you'd wait a lifetime
no matter how many years.

But even though it seems so long,
two years is just a while.
We'll have a lifetime
to joke, to laugh, and to smile.

So just remember this my darling
and keep a happy smile,
I'll love you for a lifetime
and that's longer than awhile .

On This Mountain

All the lights in the darkness
give off a glow.
From up here on this mountain,
I see the world below.

It's different from my little mountain
with the horses and the river.
Life is sometimes very complex,
I contemplate with a shiver.

I dream about sharing mountains
and hope it could be so.
But I know that wherever life leads,
I will gladly go.

For up on my mountain,
I can clearly see.
Possessions are not my focus;
love holds the key.

My key and my future
I'll happily give.
For smiles of joy, tranquility, and love
are all I need to live.

So take this heart and plant it
on His mountain up above,
and He will cause it to grow
an everlasting love.

Can I Enrich Your Life?

As the sun rises each morning, my desire
is to see the smile that resides within.
My joy and enthusiasm are created by you.
I want to change the heart of the world, but where shall we begin?

Two

Roses are red;
the sky is blue.
The sun, rising up,
makes diamonds from dew.

Think of good times
when you see this morning dew,
good times to cherish;
I smile while thinking of you.

The sun rises higher
and melts away the dew,
but the rose, a reminder,
I'll always love you.

I believe new life rises
from the sun and the dew,
but God must be willing
and I know it takes two.

True Love

As we embraced, I looked into your eyes,
the windows of your heart, and read its pages -
a book of love's purity and life's understanding.
Though unread for a time, I saw the wisdom of the ages.

I felt something that I never have before felt
and may never feel again - true love;
I am thankful for that moment.
Most will never know this feeling; you are my dove.

I want you to know because of that moment
I now feel life's contentment,
and though that heart is chained by another,
I feel no resentment.

Only love, it's life's true meaning
and cannot be measured.
Your gift to me, a moment in time,
that page from the book of your heart, will always be treasured.

As time passes, I long for your touch,
to hear your voice, to see your smiling face.
I smile, for that moment revealed to me
the meaning of life, true love, and God's grace.

The Covey

Eight birds make up this new covey,
a special gift, a new home.
Preparation for their freedom,
a new mountain for them to roam.

Nesting high above the valley floor,
sit these birds of a feather.
A cedar home for them to live,
secure from the weather.

Safe and out of harm's way,
fed by a loving hand.
This little covey of quail
will be a happy band.

They'll mate there and hatch their young
up on their new mountain.
They'll scratch for seeds and scurry about
and bathe there in the fountain.

Then, as the sun rises each spring day,
we'll hear their special call, "Bob-white!"
and know that we have shared
with them another enchanted night.

Freedom is for real,
and love is as the sun.
A warm desire to form a covey
where you and I are one.

Questions of the Heart

Where are you -
a view from someone else's eye?
Take heed, I see the questions in your heart.
Yours to answer, not mine, but not another's lies.

For another cannot understand what you ask
or see what your heart demands.
Nor can another walk in your shoes for even a while
as you advance to your mountain high.

Suffer the desert of your life,
your heart so parched and dry.
The emptiness of life and loss,
no feeling left inside except to cry.

Where are you -
a view from someone else's eye?

Special Vacation

I'd love to take a special trip
to share my dreams with you
just to be with you and be happy
and do what we must do.

To feel the warm sand between our toes,
to hold hands, to smile, and play.
Run together in the surf and sun.
To experience the beauty together each day.

Then when this trip is over,
our return to rainy weather,
we'll know if we are to part
or forever be together.

We'll know if we are to love,
we'll know if we are to hate,
we'll know if we can salvage this marriage,
we'll know if it's too late.

But whatever life brings us,
this trip will help us to prepare.
We'll be together for one week
to see if we can care.

To find out if love is real,
I believe, this, we must do
for you to believe me when I say
"My lady, I do love you."

Your Smile

T'was a time in life
when all was not so grand.
Then you appeared and
gently took my hand.

A touch so soft and caring
directly from your heart.
The heart, so pure,
the only place to start.

Your warm smile brought back
all things that are real.
Life, love, and happiness,
bonded with a kiss, the seal.

Whether it was our choice
or our fate,
the chance belongs to us;
life's offer is never late.

I'll take that hand, your touch,
a kiss, a smile.
We'll live this life together,
as we journey all the while.

Embracing on our travels
as we hold each other's hand.
We'll share throughout eternity
in God's promise land.

Picture Angel

A picture of an angel,
it's you darling that I see.
A picture of my angel,
here in front of me.

The way I want to see you,
loving eyes, a beautiful smile,
as if you're saying, "I'll love you
and not just for awhile."

But is this the way I'll see you,
or will I see you at all?
Yes, will my angel be there
when I come home this fall?

Then again, I see your picture
only this time up above.
Background in a pale blue sky,
a picture of my love.

As sweat trickles across my brow,
I bend slowly to my knees
praying to be with you, angel,
and this time I'll say please.

This Girl

Why does it seem so long?
A dream, a girl, my life.
Waiting for the day to come
when this girl can be my wife.

This girl to my wife, that day shall come,
and it's not so far away.
Lifelong happiness will be ours
in succeeding days.

But then I think, "Maybe this is my dream,
and you don't really see it as I."
I'm scared, shaking, and I'm afraid.
a tear comes to my eye.

And sleep comes, only to wake myself
yelling your name, love me.
Then I ask myself, this question
"My love, do you really see?"

Though I am not there
warming you with my love,
wait for me; and remember this,
"It's you, I love."

Woman

God's creation,
an exclamation
in exaltation;
my summation.

Love you.

Frames of Life

Friendship

Friendship is not an emotion
but a state of being,
a happening that occurs,
a destiny, a relative thing.

A friend is for always;
a friend is so true;
a friend is there to help
when love has left you blue.

A friend is there to help you
whenever you have a need,
no emotion needed,
just to take the lead.

To guide you through your
darkest stormy hours,
protect you from the lighting,
shield you from the showers.

To give all they have,
to mend a broken heart,
to pick you up when you fall,
and give a brand new start.

As my friends shared
their destiny with me,
my state of being improved;
I'm okay, I can see.

So thank you for your friendship;
I'll cherish it until the end.
Know that if you're ever down,
I'll always be your friend.

From My Eyes

Life is too short
so every passing moment should be cherished.
Every tick of the clock should be
greeted with a smile.

Do you wonder why I rush?
It's the uncertainty of life.
So much to do
and yet, so little time.

The reality is I'm moving too fast,
but I can't slow down.
Join me or step aside
for I must live fast.

Love unconditionally,
give without measure,
and never look back
for the light is at the end.

Spiraling

Seeking the best life has to offer,
each day is a quest.
But knowing all things have a price,
I still seek the best.

Work hard; play hard.
Take time to rest.
Climb the highest mountain.
Life is unchecked.

A hand extended from heaven,
take hold and be blessed.

Life provides no guarantees
along the quest;
we often fall short of our goal,
never attaining the best.

We work hard; we play hard
with no time to rest.
Looking up from this valley,
life is unchecked.

Reach up to heaven;
take hold, and be blessed.

When I'm heavy hearted with no
direction or pursuit,
I feel that I settle for mediocrity,
and I can't have what's due.

I work hard, too tired to play,
and there's no time to rest.
In the muck and the mire,
"Why?" seems to embody life's only test.

I can't reach up.
I just cry out to be blessed.

At the end of life's quest,
never attaining the best,
I stood life's test, it's time now,
I rest .and cry out, "By death, I am blessed."

Relationships

Life as we live it is an experience;
learning more about relationships enrich it as we go.
Sad thing, this journey,
we loose the ones we love as we go.

Without Bounds

My love knows no bounds;
my heart lives in the manger.
My mind takes over
when my heart is in danger.

I have not always been so fortunate.
There were times in my past
when love left it's scar
and forever didn't last.

So, if I seem distant
or maybe down hearted about life,
here's why. A man needs to be number one
in the eyes of a woman, his wife.

Never again do I want to venture there
unless I know for sure.
The scar's always there; it's tender, and it hurts too much.
Indeed, there is no cure.

A Twig in a Park

I stand on this earth
as a small twig in a park,
surrounded, but yet all alone,
a stranger in the dark.

Seeking only to increase my knowledge
and to preserve my well being,
or as it is stated by many others,
just to do my own thing.

But as the sprout fights all resistance
in its fight to become a mighty tree,
I struggle to endure life's hardships
in the search for a better me.

I have made it this far
along life's rocky road.
While the tree stands tall and strong
withstanding pressure, I'm free, I'm bold.

I stand upon my rock;
a mass of blank faces I see,
wondering why I'd yield my life
so that others might always be free.

I don't know why, but I'll be forgotten
as the stranger in the dark,
as the fallen oak will be replaced
by another twig somewhere in a park.

Moratorium 1969

Echoing through the mass of faces
came the words "love and peace."
Demanding for the world to listen,
their plea, a cry, for war to cease.

"Will someone hear this lonesome cry?"
the people's voices say.
Without young men, destruction will come;
our land, America, will decay.

They are the pride of this nation;
please bring them home today.
Is your heart so cold and bitter
that you can turn or back away?

Away from a weary father, a mother,
a sister, a brother, a heartbroken wife.
Only asking for one thing
a son, a brother, a husband, his life.

It's true that you can turn and walk,
shrug you shoulders, grin and say, "Oh, well."
We'll show you, we'll march for peace;
we'll riot; and we'll raise some hell.

Until your mind changes
and you bring them home,
stand like a president
but stand alone.

Newel's Journey

I traveled the roads of life as a man,
seeking adventure along the way,
living the dreams of freedom,
making the most of each day.

I shared with many
the tales of my youth, challenging life with no fear,
breaking horses, blazing trails, and
providing for those that I held so dear.

I leave you with memories of
good things and of my love for you,
the times we shared around the fire -
yes, some fiction, but mostly true.

I'll miss those times of sharing
my life with you and you with me.
But know this as you taste your heavenly chocolate,
it's sweeter than this life, you'll see.

There's just a little more.
I left you with a kiss of love
but didn't finish my journal.
Don't forget the chocolate when you join me in life's eternal.

Remember

Nothing is certain,
and life doesn't last very long.
So on your face, keep a smile
and in your heart, a song.

Remember, when life challenges you
in word, in thought, or deed,
your song and smile may disappear
and leave you there in need.

In need of someone warm
to hold your hand and say,
"Remember when we used to laugh?
We'll do it again someday."

Remember only the good things
of the one who left today.
A tough man, a good heart,
a desert rat, you say.

When you cry and cry
to wash away the pain,
sometimes the tears, a few
and sometimes tears, like rain.

Unchecked and untreated, the pain
will turn your heart to stone.
So rid yourself of this plague,
and let your life go on.

But until that day, our job is
as plain as it can be,
to remind the ones we love
about eternity.

The time won't be long for life is short;
He'll greet us with His Son.
He'll show us what forever is;
we'll smile and sing along.

To live each day as if our last,
to joke, to laugh, and to smile,
to share our love and happiness,
to touch, to love, a kiss, a while.

Friends

I hear a voice of wisdom;
I am thankful I've been enriched.
We shared a few moments together;
our paths became entrenched.
I am thankful I now know the trust of another.

A Callous or a Tear?

The question,
"What does the future hold?
The answer, "Am I to be meek
or aggressive and bold?"

"Do I turn over the rocks
or let them lie?"
"Should I be calloused,
and withhold the tear in my eye?"

USS Portland CA -33

The brave men who rode upon my decks were grand
in service to their country,
divisions, groups, officers, and all -
a team hand in hand.

We left our first port shiny and new,
the men and I, on February 23, 1933.
Some gave all; all gave their best
as we toiled for our country upon the sea.

God granted me thirteen years of service;
many shipmates staffed and joined me during those years.
I loved you all, as you did me;
with all of you, I laughed and shed so many tears.

Thank you one and all, from captain to seaman;
your time was my blessing and my joy.
Through war and peace we rode
the wave together, both man and boy.

At sea you had many names.
I was proud of mine - "Sweet Pea."
You fought the enemy bravely; some died.
They are now with me.

No more war as we sail
by God's grace, you see.
Our spirit will live on
as we sail upon His sea.

Though my decks are only memories
in the mind of a few,
you, who walked my decks in life,
come and join me as my crew.

Fireside Reflections

A quiet evening by the fire,
deep thought transpires,
reflecting on life
and daily desires.

From the heart,
understanding must come,
of friendship before love,
never felt by some.

Let your heart take the lead,
purge your thoughts of lust.
Now waltz to this rhythm,
a friend one can trust.

The race of life plays
with no beginning or end.
Gone the desire to conquer,
forever, this fire, my friend.

Embrace from the heart;
find truth in friendship, love, compassion, and sharing.
Caress the hearts of all that you meet
with true understanding and caring.

Steamboat Inn on the Umpqua

White water, an evergreen forest,
beauty only the imagination can comprehend.
Melting snowflakes from high above,
sculpting and carving in nature's way.

Imagine, if you will, a river;
enjoy the beauty, sit for awhile.
The fluid nectar of the mountains cascading down and sweeping past,
creating a never ending work of art.

Always beautiful,
never complete,
the Master's touch is awesome;
we try but cannot compete.

Experience the Umpqua
from the decks of the Steamboat Inn;
knock at the innkeeper's door
for they will let you in.

Feel your burdens lift
as you ascend the rocky path,
or cleanse your soul with rod and reel
in nature's perfect bath.

Cast your fly behind that rock
where the steel head lie.
Watch the eagle as he searches
from his perch on high.

Listened to the elk's mating call
as you taste the grapes of the mountain.
Inhale the wild flowers' fragrance
and feel the mist from the river's fountain.

Imagine a river, the Umpqua, is real;
walk the path; let the forest take you in.
Taste its life; stop and knock
at the door of the Steamboat Inn.

My Cozy Little Nest

The world belongs to me,
here in my cozy little nest.
I feel a sense of security tonight
as I settle down to rest.

I have turned my back on emptiness;
it's time I start to live.
Life has a lot to offer,
and I have a lot to give.

You opened up my eyes,
and now it is you I see.
The joy this life has
I see here, from my nest.

With the knowledge that all is well,
I am ready to begin.
Thank you for that awareness
and the peace that lies within.

Because you opened up your heart,
I do know, now, I am blessed.
As I smile and close my eyes,
I think of you and rest.

Kindness and Happiness

There are many people with only one
thought, to be living.
Thinking only of themselves,
not too kind nor too forgiving.

Who has yet to learn the
meaning of life -
the fulfillment of dreams and
the meaning of right,

the right thing to do while
trying to be fair,
the decisions to make when the
right times are there?

To find out today what life
really means to you,
To appreciate life, there are two
things that you must do.

Be kind to family and friends while
you are still at home.
You never realize what they mean
until they are gone.

Live not only for yourself
but for the happiness of others each day.
Someone dear may leave you, and
tomorrow can take them away.

Musings

Day To Day Dreams

It seems that I've missed the boat somewhere in life.
"I just want to be your friend." Never had one for a wife.
My friends always loved another; I really must be a louse.
I'll never marry again, I'll find one who hates me and buy them a house.

I'll be your Huckleberry; and I'll be your friend, but I'm a little lazy.
I'm hot, don't touch me, I chase grizzlies and could be crazy.
I ain't no daisy; I run with the wolves and talk to the elk, a mountain man.
I need a Bigfoot wife, a woman from the wild who understands who I am.

She'll love me in the treetops and down by the river.
No house to clean, that's nature's way. The thought makes me shiver.
We'll propagate the species, a wild mountain man and a bigfoot wife.
We'll lie beneath the redwoods as we contemplate our life.

She won't say much as I climb to kiss those big ole lips.
She'll slam me to the ground and pin me with those big ole hips.
We'll have a bunch of children; she'll teach them how to swing.
I'll write bigfoot ballads and teach them how to sing.

I'm headed to the mountains; no more houses for me.
No more courts and orders; I'll be as happy as can be.
My friends will be the animals; my nourishment, the vine.
Hey, vintner, pour me another glass of wine.

Directions

Little steps, little pages,
savor the way.
Learn to love;
live today.

Experience
the joy of the game
that never ends
nor stays the same.

Red to stop,
green is okay.
Leo says
Gemini can play.

The book of life,
the team of Mom and Dad.
With little steps,
you will be glad.

Like the tide
throughout the ages,
we learn from history
on little pages.

Little steps
we've taken
here and
through the ages.

To trust, to honor, and to obey -
directions etched in stone and little pages;
The Word is written
to find His way.

Okay

Why do we do things that we do
that we don't really mean to do?
We do them because we want to
and that, we'll always do.

And if it's because we want to,
then that's what we should do.
And if it's okay with you, too,
that's what I shall do.

But if I do
something that I didn't really mean to do,
I'll say I did it
because I wanted to.

Today

Today is the first day
of the rest of your life.
Does that mean a brighter day
free from trouble and strife?

Or is today another day
just like the day before
with empty rooms and empty hearts?
What really lies in store?

Like waves on a deserted beach,
no one to see or care,
wasted effort to shape the sand
because no one's there.

We sweat and work,
what is our plight?
Little do we gain.
The sun is hot; the air is dry. It's driving me insane.

A raindrop of hope comes
falling down from the blue sky above.
A vision appeared before my eyes,
the One who has the gift of love.

He spoke, "I give you this gift of love,
share it with those in need.
Give them hope and inspiration
in word and thought and deed."

Then each day will have meaning
much brighter than the day before,
and no one will ask,
for they will know what tomorrow has in store.

Tomorrow

Why is it that tomorrow
seems so far away
that I cannot see it
as I see it today?

Is it that force
has blocked my view,
or is there a tomorrow
for me or for you?

I am not certain,
but this I will say,
"There is no tomorrow
only a preceding day."

This statement is true
of the succeeding day.
There is no tomorrow.
It's always today.

This is the reason,
"A truth!" I'll say,
"It can't be predicted
it's too far away."

A Lady with Dark Hair

All things in perspective,
though not always what they seem,
I make it through the days by hard work,
but at night I dream.

Muffins and bagels on a platter,
fresh peaches and cream,
breakfast for two,
a lady with dark hair, I dream.

The white sand, the morning sea breeze,
the palm trees, and me.
"Port in two hours,"
the speakers echo in a scream.

The sun, warm upon my back,
a tropical drink, something and cream.
As I embrace my companion and smell the fragrance of the flowers,
I scream.

She feels a lot like my pillow!
Things are not always as they seem.
For breakfast, shall I have muffins and bagels
or peaches and cream?

Or maybe just coffee and toast,
nothing too extreme.
Go to work to pass the day;
for tonight, I can dream.

Fear Not

Successes and failures are recorded in history
so as not to travel the wrong road twice,
but always a mystery when
de je vou turns out so nice.

Life is not an equation,
and it's not a game.
For the same outcome,
all circumstances and players must have the same name.

Fear not when you enter
what seems not new.
This stage was set
just for you.

Participate in life's play;
don't be timid; give it your all.
Belief assures us a happy ending,
just make that curtain call.

Aged to Perfection

Hello, I'm down here aging in this large vat.
I'll send a message in a bottle to be placed under your mat.

"Read the message," it will say, "I'm turning old to new.
I'm waiting here, I hear your voice, I belong to you."

I've heard the words "I love you"; I know, in fact, it's true;
I'll wait, for I belong to you.

As you sip from my glass, I know you will be mine.
Though at this moment I'm but a grape, I'll make the best wine.

There will be no wine before it's time; I shall pass the test,
When you come to take me home, I'll taste the very best.

Rocks

Everything needs to be wanted;
we all have needs,
basking in the sunshine
between the white line and the weeds.

Last winter when the snow was on,
they dumped us guys all out.
We kept you safe on your highway travels;
that's what our life's about.

But now I lie beside the road
and watch as you go by.
I feel a sense of emptiness;
but rocks, they just don't cry.

I'm praying for the snow again
as I lie here with these seeds.
I know it won't be long until
I'm on your list of needs.

Good Morning

I just wanted to say good morning
as I go about my day,
being happy, living life, counting all my blessings
all along the way.

Thank you for being here
in my thoughts as I play,
hoping to be in your thoughts
if it causes you to smile and have a great day.

Blowing Kisses

Hello, I see you are away.
Just calling to brighten up your day.

I am blowing kisses from far away.
Hope you felt my presence sometime today.

If one of my kisses found its way,
just wanted to know if you could play.

Answer Butler

Hello, I answer for Jim when he is away;
I tell him only the things you ask me to say.

Please leave a message, so that I can play
when he returns at the end of the day.

The Love Card

Thank you for depositing a lifetime of love in such a short period of time.
As a cardholder, you may use your new Love Card, the Littlepage, at
anytime to withdraw from your account.

And I am pleased to inform you that no matter how much you take out you
will never deplete the supply. You are, therefore, a lifetime cardholder of
the Littlepage and are encouraged to make regular withdrawals to keep the
account manageable.

As a cardholder, you are also eligible for many other benefits, please
contact the manager of this account for details.

The Littlepage Card Manager

It's Love, My Luv

For years I was nothing
in the eyes of my Luv.
To realize it sooner would have been better;
it was not I, the louse, a bum.

But those who came before me
set the mold for the shoes I wore,
self-centered and deceitful,
only of themselves did they care for.

Many wounds did I bear, many scars did appear
slanting Luv's view.
Unable to give Love,
Luv, herself, became the shrew.

I needed Luv, but Love I needed, too.
With Luv and without Love, I became like those I detest,
self-serving, disrespectful, and wicked.
You know the rest.

No justification,
only pain and shame,
I must confess,
the louse, I became.

Soiled and tarnished,
a disgrace to my name,
mortally wounded,
my spirit was lamed.

Choices, choices,
I became
another looser
in life's deadly game.

Yet, God's light
allowed me to see
His love, a love
He has there for me.

The blood of Jesus cleansed my soul
and my sin.
I opened the gate,
and His love flooded in.

The reflection,
the choice,
no longer a louse,
time to rejoice.

Love everlasting
now flows through me
to my Luv.
Because I Loved, I am set free.

The Watcher

I go to bed with the bats and get up with the birds;
am I a vampire bat or an eagle?
Though I am no one's canine, I'm stealth like a wolf;
but I am loyal and love like a beagle.

I am your protector and your friend;
I'm your safety net,
your guardian in the night,
for it is my set.

You will never see me
unless you should become prey.
I will devour the rodents that hurt you
for it is my stay.

I'm not truly an eagle or a wolf,
but I have a job to do.
I was the guardian angel of another;
he'll be here too.

But for now I join hands with others
to protect his dream.
He is the eagle and the wolf, all things feigned,
not to be as they seem.

A Wave

The rustle of wind,
a wave, a pounding heart,
an infant is borne,
a wave, a breath, the start.

The wind blows harder,
the wave grows longer,
more breaths are taken,
a heart grows stronger.

The wind brings a violent storm,
waves in a flurry.
Faster beats the pounding heart,
someone's in a hurry.

The wave's last ripple
just before coming on shore,
the last step taken,
the heart beats no more.

Pendulum

Each day passes
just as a new day begins.
The pendulum swings back and forth,
back and forth, it never ends.

Life is a line curved, like that of a circle,
or straight, the distance between two shapes;
neither round or even,
it begins, but it never ends, early or late.

So take heed; some things are real.
Some fake, all are not fair.
Seek the truth, learn, and realize;
no matter where you are, you're there.

Home is where the heart is,
and life doesn't last very long.
Take a homeless heart; build a dream;
fill the rebel's empty song.

Each day passes as the day before.
Should one ask, "Who are you?"
"A dreamer," I would say,
"And you?"

"A realist, yes?" Nothing is ever certain,
but life ends quickly as the bird's song.
Down life's lonely road,
it sometimes seems so long.

The circle can be broken;
the line comes to an end.
The pendulum moves to the other side,
just as a new day begins.

Seasons

Christmas Truth

Listening to the voices within my heart,
I find truth in the Christmas season,
a celebration of the birth of
our Lord and Savior, Jesus Christ,
the Son of God, the Prince of Peace.

We look for the perfect gift to express our love
as a reminder of His perfect Gift to us, the Son, our Savior.

Biblical truth, written for us to follow;
I know God made all things great and small.
He gave life to Adam and Eve,
but Satan entered and caused them to sin.

We look for the perfect gift to express our love
as a reminder of His perfect Gift to us, the Son, our Savior.

Christmas Reflections

The joy I experienced on Christmas eve
left little to wonder, what do I believe?
I believe all things were created by His hands
and all things happen according to his plans.

His son Jesus came and died for my soul;
because of his love and my repentance, I am now whole.
Reflections of new life, His promise, my joy,
all made possible by God's little boy.

Born on Christmas day so very long ago,
Joseph, Mary, and God, I'm sure, loved Him so.
The hope that was born in the manger that day,
a beam in the darkness to light up our way.

Written words for us to follow from that Christmas past
gives meaning to life, true love that lasts.
All that He asks is to make Him our choice.
We'll know life's true meaning when we hear His voice.

Christmas Gift

God's creation, all that we know,
the stars in the sky, the new fallen snow.

Each day His day, by grace we live.
His Word received, for us to also give.

He sent His Son on Christmas day,
love's sacrifice washed our sins away.

He gave up this life, a Gift heaven sent.
To receive life everlasting, we must repent.

Live in the joy of Christmas each day.
Accept this Gift; for all, I kneel to pray.

Experience the joy; surrender to His love;
then share the Gift from heaven above.

Christmas Love

For the hearts of this world, Jesus came so very long ago,
born out of God's love for us, in truth, no doubt, I know.

Born in a manger in Bethlehem so very long ago,
His star lit up the way to heaven, in truth, no doubt, it's so.

He lived His life in purity so very long ago;
He modeled love and spoke of life eternal, in truth, no doubt, I know.

He gave up His life on the cross, so very long ago;
His cleansing blood set us free, in truth, no doubt, it's so.

In prayer, I thank Him for the gift of life this Christmas day.
The Bible is the guiding light; His love paves the way.

Christmas Garden

God has given me a life
with many eventful times
filled with great joy.
But in Christmas times, He gives
each of us a very special gift
of planting the seed of eternal love in the garden of our heart.

The seeds are all the same when planted. They are
tender but resilient, needing water,
fertilizer, and cultivation to grow strong.
My promise is
that I will be the gardener and
caretaker of this very special gift.

I will do all things
possible through Him; I will cultivate,
fertilize, spray, prune, and constantly
monitor the garden of our love.
It will be filled with many beautiful flowers and the
fragrance of our love will last forever.

Merry Christmas.

Christmas Shopping

So many people are shopping for Christmas presents today;
it's a tradition, the day after Thanksgiving.
The sales, the crowds, and the traffic, all for that special gift
to light the eyes of a child, the joy of giving.

Okay, where is my list? It's got to be here somewhere;
Found it! An action toy for Alyscia, Carson's first baseball and bat.
Hear the Christmas music, taste the cookies, smell the evergreens,
and Santa Claus . . . , but wait. Elf's aren't supposed to look like that.

This is all great fun, but I can't wait to get together
with family and friends on that special day.
The day we as Christians choose to celebrate God's gift of life to us,
His Son Jesus, Happy Birthday.

A gift so great yet tragic; He gave His Son for us.
The tears He must have shed.
It's all about the love He has for you and I,
Jesus's blood to cleanse us, the Christmas suit of white and red.

In the majesty of this season, my reflections of loved ones
at times brings sadness so great it overcomes the joy.
Because we do not know what the future holds, I pray that you
accept the gift of life made possible by God's little Boy.

Then celebrate your gift of everlasting life on this the day of our Lord,
Christmas Day, the twenty-fifth day of December, two thousand and two.
And walk each day with the Prince of Peace, for God created you,
Jesus saves you, the Holy Spirit guides you; all three in one,
They love you.
Merry Christmas.

125

Christmas Prayer

Our Father,

The day is Christmas,
the smile of joy,
the love of God, the Son,
His boy.

His life for us,
this Christmas birthday,
born to wash
our sins away.

Thank you, God.
His life, the Gift,
Your love and His,
my spirits lift.

The day is Christmas.
Jesus, God's grace,
my debt to Him,
He took my place.

Happy Birthday, Jesus.
We'll do it your way.
Oh, the joy of living
on this Christmas day.

Christmas Treasure

"Merry Christmas,"
I say
with joy
in my heart.

"Merry Christmas, my dear,
I miss you tonight."
Oh, to be with you,
and all would be right.

The peace you have given
is far beyond measure.
I seek not gold or jewels
for you are my treasure.

Oh, to be with you
on this Christmas day.
Your smile lights the darkness
to show me the way.

Easter

The beginning of new life,
warm sunshine, the dogwoods, and daffodil.
Experiencing rebirth,
oh, such a thrill.

Know there is truth and meaning;
taste the fruits of life.
Live in happiness daily
free from the routine and strife.

Feel the warm sunshine
and smell the fresh flowers.
Witness the beauty of the clouds,
and feel the April showers.

The new life that spring brings
is not there by chance.
God gave us this time of year
to watch our spirit dance.

He gave us His Son's blood
to cleanse us from our sins,
a way to open the gate
and let our Savior in.

Easter is a time for celebration,
of new life and great things.
Imagine, if you will, a paradise,
what life after death can bring.

Thank you for springtime,
fresh flowers and warm sunshine,
and the knowledge, by saying yes,
that all these things will be mine.

Resurrection of Faith

Today, an Easter Sunday,
the date of the resurrection of Jesus Christ,
I prayed, I waited patiently,
God spoke to my heart.

My direction was not His
but mine, destined for hell.
I stopped. "Show me the way, Lord."
He spoke clearly and quietly, "Follow me."

"I thought I was," I said.
"Open up your eyes," His reply.
"Be certain of your path, My Word.
Demons will shade the way.

"It is their mission to deliver your soul to Satan.
Wake up. Repent.
Set your eyes on the Light.
Follow me," again He said.

"Make My words your thoughts.
Make My words your deeds.
If you get lost, stop and pray.
I will answer.

"It's all up to you.
Follow me,"
again He said.
"Be reborn."

Pleasures of Autumn

by Grandpa Rufus Littlepage

In the early days of Autumn
when the leaves begin to fall
and the breeze becomes quite chilly,
it's refreshing to us all.

The burning heat of summer
is giving fast away
making room for a different season
that will bring a cooler day.

The trees with acorns are loaded
and other nuts of various kinds
supplying food for many birds
and also food for swine.

The crows are densely swarming;
hear their beckoning call,
"Hurry, hurry, hurry.
There is plenty for us all."

On come the squirrels and chipmunks;
they seemed to be filled with glee.
You can hear them joyfully squeaking
as they jump from tree to tree.

Oh, here comes Mister Hunter
with his dogs and gun.
It may interfere with those harvest hands;
he will put them on the run.

They will hide in hollow trees
with their hearts so full of sorrow
thinking over what has happened,
but they will be back tomorrow.

The thrilling joy of school days
is felt by everyone.
All the children are so happy
that school has begun.

Beautiful are the mountain sides
arrayed in colors so gay.
Manifesting the many wondrous charms
of a pleasant autumn day.

Seasons of Death

Death is a dogwood in the spring
where the green grass grows and the red bird sings.

In the summer, death is a flower
cooled by rain from a midday shower.

Death in autumn, is like winded leaves in the sky
as a formation of geese slowly glide by.

But in the winter, death, when it snows,
is a lonely, lonely valley where nobody goes.